Behind The
**BIG
RED
DOOR**

Behind The

BIG
RED
DOOR

From Trauma To Success—
Personally, Professionally, And Spiritually

Angela Webber
(Angie Kay)

INDIE BOOKS
INTERNATIONAL

Behind The BIG RED DOOR

From Trauma To Success—*Personally, Professional, And Spiritually*

Paperback ISBN: 978-1-966168-18-8
Hardback ISBN: 978-1-966168-20-1
Library of Congress Control Number: 2025906599

Designed by Melissa Farr, Back Porch Creative, LLC

INDIE BOOKS INTERNATIONAL®, INC.
2511 WOODLANDS WAY
OCEANSIDE, CA 92054
www.indiebooksintl.com

This is the true joy in life, the being used for a purpose recognized by yourself as a mighty one; the being a force of nature instead of a feverish, selfish little clod of ailments and grievances complaining that the world will not devote itself to making you happy.

I am of the opinion that my life belongs to the whole community, and as long as I live it is my privilege to do for it whatever I can.

I want to be thoroughly used up when I die, for the harder I work, the more I live. I rejoice in life for its own sake. Life is no "brief candle" to me. It is sort of a splendid torch which I have got hold of for the moment, and I want to make it burn as brightly as possible before handing it on to future generations.

GEORGE BERNARD SHAW, "A SPLENDID TORCH"

Contents

Foreword   ix

Preface   1

Chapter 1   Two Families Become Three   5
Chapter 2   Freedom Isn't Free   17
Chapter 3   Emotions   27
Chapter 4   Knickknacks On The Shelf   35
Chapter 5   The Cycle Of A Relationship   45
Chapter 6   Five Degrees Of A Customer   51
Chapter 7   Success Starts With You   61

Acknowledgments   *81*
About The Author   *85*
Author's Notes   *87*
Praise From A Friend   *89*
Works Cited   *91*

Foreword

As a clinical neuropsychologist, I observe the importance of mental health in the workplace and in family life on a daily basis. When I earned my PhD from Georgia State University, I had the ambition to improve people's lives by better understanding the power of neuropsychology. In my role as a leadership coach and mentor to high-performance teams, I cannot overstate the importance of the right mental attitude.

In today's society, we are socialized and taught to deal with negative emotions in one of two ways: (a) push them down, suppress them, and hide them away from ourselves and others; (b) let them flow freely as you wish, spewing toxic negativity everywhere. Neither of these approaches is healthy for us as individuals or our society.

Author Angie Webber, through her unique writing style, captures the topic in a way no academic or self-help book can. She lets the reader experience her thoughts, feelings, and actions in a unique and effective way. And her message shows the way to a better approach to dealing with emotions. It is not an approach of struggling to hide them or spewing them forth, but one of managing them in ways that are adaptive rather than maladaptive.

As Angie points out, our response to our emotions is our responsibility. We get to decide whether to bring calm or anger to the storm. While Angie comes at the issue of managing emotions from a layperson's perspective, and we would not agree on every point she makes, I respect the passion she has for the subject, and her main message is spot-on and accurate. As she points out, processing our emotions and learning to manage them takes time and requires hard work.

For the person who wants to better themself and manage their mindset, self-examination of our hearts and our minds is a necessary tool. Thanks, Angie, for sounding this alarm and sharing your insights on the importance of managing emotions.

Steve Swavely, PhD
Founder and president of Evolution Leadership Coaching, author of *Ignite Your Leadership*

Preface

In customer service, we don't often take life into consideration. What makes individuals react the way they do, or what helps them to be more satisfied and comfortable working with us? The baggage that comes with interacting with the public, co-workers, and bosses can cause us to lose opportunities for success.

The scariest part of opening the Big Red Door is seeing what lies behind it. Having the courage to lay out all the internal struggles means pulling down that handle to peek behind it. We are often surprised to find this is where all the hopes and dreams that we longed for were hidden.

All the years of hiding the hurts and fears that traumatic emotions left behind, we find a new path to journey where we can process the isolation of loneliness from hiding, our bleeding hearts and broken spirits from the sharp tongues and bruises from the blows that life dished out so willingly.

My own journey in its raw state, while sad, was the beginning of all the life lessons that I would need to find my success. The trauma I endured gave me the drive to continue to push past all the smoke and mirrors of deceit to find the success that is purposed for my life's ambitions.

The emotions that dwell right under the surface of our flesh are one of the keys to success. Sharing how I championed the challenges that tried to hold me back can empower us to find our success by leaning on the techniques I will share.

Understanding trauma and how it affects us and those around us will guide us through the difficulty of emotions and how to harness them so that the battles we fight to hold ourselves together will not hold us back or cause us to hold back others from finding their true success in life.

Many will stay stuck in the world of emotional battles; however, they need the courage to step out and away from all the lies and misinformation, from self-help information, and find better ways to meet those battles head-on and deal with them personally.

The only person that I can control is me. So, no matter what challenge arises, we must try our hardest to keep control of the emotions that arise, keeping the emotions within us neatly organized and in place so when the occasion arises, we are ready with our best response.

Most importantly, in business and the area of understanding those in these traps of life where emotions are overbearing and controlling a person's responses, it becomes important to be able to respond appropriately. When in the social spaces of life, work, friends, or even family, we find ourselves battling within to keep the balance that we so desperately long for.

Businesses are not prepared to meet the challenges for their customers or staff who face these challenges. As the world shifts more and more to the offhand technologies for customer service, they are not willing to recognize the challenges on both sides of the counter, for their staff or customers.

Life is always in balance, from personal to business and spiritual. We need the compass of all three to guide us in the right direction so that we can not only be successful ourselves but so that we bring as many with us as possible.

Finding the courage to pull down that handle so the door can open and digging deeper into the root of that which keeps us from success will be the best decision you can make for yourself, your family, professionally, and for the peace that comes from within your spirit. Join me as we find success.

Angela Webber
Virginia

Greater love hath no man than this,
that a man lay down his life for his friends.

JOHN 15:13

Chapter 1

When Two Families Become Three

My biological parents began our family under the stressful conditions of an unplanned pregnancy. It would be years before I came onto the scene; however, by then, much of the damage had been done. The absence of parenting and guidance from their individual families left them ill-equipped to manage family life.

This was especially true of my biological mother. I don't believe from the stories that I have heard that she was prepared to be married and a mom living the day-to-day expectations of what a housewife would require. She began to leave after the second child was born, and for periods of time, she took my two older brothers with her.

Her family struggled with alcohol abuse and other mental and emotional challenges throughout her childhood that I believe caused her to want more from life than feeling stuck in a typical home life. I never had the pleasure of meeting her or any of my extended family from her side after she had left for the last time.

My father's father passed away when he was only three. Growing up without the male role model he would need to guide him through marriage and family life left him working hard to find solutions to help make the relationship work, however, to no avail.

My father's mom, Nana, a widow at a very early age, worked as a nurse and managed to buy a little house that I adored. It was a small two-bedroom, one-bath with a half kitchen. It was so tiny. I believe it was only seven hundred square feet. She grew a peach tree and a grapevine in her tiny backyard, and the smell of gardenias permeated her screened porch. I can still smell the squash plants growing in her garden. She hosted many pastors in her home in Georgia alongside her family and was a firm believer in the protection of deity. She had turned her little backyard into a small Georgia plantation and lived there for many decades while raising and supporting my dad until she became too feeble to live alone. She never re-married because she believed she should be the wife of one man and didn't want another man to come in and hurt her son.

I still cherish all the Saturday nights when it was my turn to spend the night with her. We had so much fun, and I shared her heart for growing plants and quilting, and we bonded over many crafts. She filled in the gaps of life by giving me a safe place to lay my head, if even for a night. She helped where she could and always seemed to enjoy us tagging along with her. She never drove a car, so we learned how to take buses and took many walks.

I have no recollection of meeting any of my biological mother's family. I know of a grandmother and an aunt; however, I have no memory of any of them or of my biological mother. I have been asked often why I don't go find them. I have peace in understanding that her life may be good, and if she chooses not to make the effort to be a part of us, then pushing to be a part of her could cause her harm, and I choose to refrain from doing that.

The Hard Days

As I have previously mentioned, my biological mother really struggled with her current state. She left for periods of time and would travel with my two older brothers. I find it interesting that she would take us kids on these "adventures"; however, I believe it shows that she must have had some sense of responsibility.

On one of the occasions when she left, tragedy struck. My second oldest brother, named after my father's father Charles, passed away without warning. It was told to me that she had gone out for some reason, and when she returned, Charles lay in his crib, deceased.

My father was notified and traveled to have the body returned to our home state for burial. Only five or six people attended, including the pastor who performed the service. It makes me sad to think that his life was not grieved by more people. I can't imagine how forsaken Dad must have felt.

Charle's passing hit him particularly hard as not only did he lose his son, but also the sting of losing his own father over again due to the namesake of Charles. My biological mom stayed around for a bit, continuing to bear more children.

The final departure came. This would be her seventh time fleeing the life my dad had attempted to provide. My dad returned home from work to find that everything had been taken. The Christmas tree, the gifts, and all the clothes and furniture were gone. Even his clothes were gone. He was only left with one panel of one curtain hanging on one window. This visual burned inside him like a fire out of control. His main emotion became rage. He had tried everything he knew, and now his kids were gone, and everything he had worked hard for. I can imagine that he feared for our lives as losing one child already left a long-lasting impression on his heart. It seemed personal; she had devastated him. She ran up all the credit card debt and cleaned out all the bank accounts, leaving him completely broken.

He contacted a lawyer and gained custody of all three of us siblings, even though he didn't know where we were. This was unprecedented, as it was in the late '60s and early '70s. The mother was almost always granted custody. My third brother was found first. Then, by chance, he ran into the lady who had me, and she had given him quite a tongue lashing that it had been so long before anyone came to get me. He explained the situation, and we were reunited.

It would be a few more weeks before finding my oldest brother. My dad received a call from the ladies my biological mother and brother were staying with, and they coordinated a time for Dad to come get him after she had left the house. My oldest brother shared years later how relieved he was seeing Dad walk up and bring him home.

She only made contact once. She requested to take me for ice cream. I was not yet one year of age at the time, and Dad, in his grace, granted her request. Panic set in immediately, as he was very concerned about whether she would return me. Gratefully, she did, and we never saw her again.

Dad's hurt and anger dripped on us like a soaked sponge. I don't believe he was even aware of the hurt that he was causing at the time, and later in life, he always apologized for those days. As adults, we were able to be filled with forgiveness and thankfulness for his protection over us. Even though it was hard, we were safe and had a warm bed and home to live in.

I was still a small child when an angel came to us. We called her Mom. They always shared funny stories of how I would not let my dad hold her hand, and I often sat in between them, staking my claim to her. The safety they represented, I am sure, was comforting and profound to feeling complete within the family unit.

It was also shared that I cried a lot as a toddler. It was assumed that I missed my biological mom, so having my angel with me settled my heart and spirit, leaving me feeling safe and loved. She took the blows and protected us often from Dad's rage.

As I grew older, I quickly learned to stay one step ahead of the outbreaks. I found peace and solace within the walls of my room, and isolation was my friend. I was not as affected by Dad's rage as my two older brothers living at home were. I recall a time when we were watching TV, and all of a sudden, my dad hit my third oldest brother in the head with a can of soda. When we asked why, he replied that it was because he was biting his nails.

These outbursts continued often, and as we got older, we avoided home and interaction with Dad. We used humor to help deflect the drip of anger. Mom was an accountability for my dad. Many of these actions did not occur when her spirit was present.

Due to all the hardships that my brothers endured, their way out was to take their anger out on me. I was the abused sibling who was often overlooked. You may be surprised to know that many sibling groups have a battered sibling. Eighty percent of youth experience some form of mistreatment by a sibling.[1] It is called the forgotten abuse. It has been stated that even therapists frequently overlook it. The emotional effects are long-lasting, even into adulthood, and often cause families to drift apart and keep their distance.

I still remember the sting of the slap to the side of my face. The pain in my side from being thrust onto the arm of the couch by my third oldest brother. He was the only one living at home at the time, so he really took a lot of the backlash being dished out.

While I was asked often about the bruises, I claimed no foul. No one knew I was hurting; they were hurting too. It was easier to keep the pain hidden within the depths of my soul. There was a time when we were all at the grocery store, and my third oldest brother slipped a pack of Life Savers into my pocket. By the time we arrived home, somehow, my parents knew that they were there, and I was accused of stealing. I received the consequences of this action that I didn't partake of.

The anger being targeted at me started to become mine. I was angry. I was innocent, yet I was receiving the punishment that a guilty child would receive. I was often set up to receive these consequences that were unfairly dished out. The abuse wasn't only physical; it was verbal and emotional. The neglect of affection from my parents left a hole in my heart, leaving me feeling rejected. I believe they did not know this, because they were in their own survival mode as well.

A New Family

I not only gained a new mom, but I also gained a great-grandma, grandparents, uncles, aunts, and cousins. My great-grandfather immigrated over from Italy; however, he passed at an early age due to a heart condition. He came here for work and met my great-grandmother, and they got married. My grandfather John married my grandmother Rose. She was from Ohio and spent a great amount of time with Great-Grandma, who taught her how to cook Italian food to perfection. She was a profound influence in my life as she, too, had a hard childhood, and I wonder if she knew how much I needed her love. Her stories of jumping on the trains to get coal for heat were so unbelievable. I just couldn't imagine it. Her sister was born with a defect, and she lost her mom to childbirth. She was raised by a single dad and other family members.

Grandad survived WWII and the Great Depression, and in doing so, he sought the comfort of heaven to save him. While in the war, he was under a truck under heavy fire and vowed to serve the Lord every day if he saved his life. He became a pastor and served in the ministry until his passing. A promise kept. The trauma of WWII would last decades. The sights he saw were embedded in his mind, and he was truly grateful for life and every moment he could impact others. From growing up in the depression, he left a profound impact of not wasting anything. He got every ounce of toothpaste out of that tube. If he didn't finish his plate, he saved every bite for another meal. Even if it were just one bite, we would have plate inspections to make sure we ate everything possible on our plates. He would not buy himself equipment that would benefit him, such as VCRs or remote-controlled TVs, so Christmas was easy for him. We kept him current with the age of technology. He loved these "toys" and never had cable television. Always the antenna with the foil on the rabbit ears.

It was interesting that my new mom's family had interacted with my dad long before they had started courting one another. My parents had started working in the same office. A mutual attraction had occurred, and a new romance for my dad was on the horizon.

Her aunt was my babysitter, her uncle was a firefighter, and when one of my dad's cars caught fire, he was the firefighter who came to put it out. His pastor was the husband of one of her aunts. He would spend Sunday afternoons with him for guidance and the male role model that was missing in his life. They attended this same church, just at different times. They didn't pass each other while there. However, it was clear that sending this angel to be our mom was proof that the hands of God were all over it. When my dad dropped us off so that he and my now mom could go out, they arrived at her aunt's house, well, it was clear that everyone knew each other.

Now, all of us were under the umbrella of love, joy, and peace. We were now being prayed over, and healing had begun. Life was becoming bearable most days. The connection between us and heaven was being built. Life was calming down, and Dad was healing. Life wasn't all bad. We had great Christmases; we were able to go to Disney World in Florida. Mom was helping Dad to rebuild emotionally, spiritually, and financially.

While the pain of a broken dad was still trickling down from time to time, we were blessed to be accepted by more than just a mom. As a family, my dad and brothers had the support of my mom's family, and we were loved and felt safe with the people around us.

I remember a time when we had to spend a few weeks with our new grandparents. Grandpa liked to sleep in, so no noise was allowed. However, Grandma was very clever to keep us busy and quiet till he was up. Grandpa took us on hikes and showed us different kinds of snakes, and there was this amazing beehive. It had to have been fifteen feet tall and about three feet wide. There was a library that had caught fire, and the remains had lots of books and this beehive. I still have many books from this library that I treasure, even though they survived rough conditions. I related to them as myself and found them worthy.

Even though life was becoming stable I still was not performing well in school. I was struggling with focus and maintaining good grades, leaving me to graduate in summer school. The loneliness became too much to bear, and I found favor in a young man. Thinking that he would be my hero, I did what I needed to in order to keep him attracted to me. I gave him myself and then found myself pregnant. My hero then rejected me, too.

My father's fears from his trauma were pressed over me, and I was pushed to abort the child. They say aborting a baby doesn't make you unpregnant; it makes you the parent of a dead baby. I was devastated. I had placed my hopes in a person that let me down. I was never able to bond with my child, and I was so devastated at my situation that I couldn't even speak up for myself. I felt no emotions at the time, completely numb, and having no control left me paralyzed emotionally.

I distinctly remember lying in the back seat when all was done. My father asked what I wanted for dinner, and I couldn't even tell you anything after that question. It was later shared with me that for about three months, I was absent emotionally. Even Christians make huge mistakes and choices that don't honor God. The great part is there is grace for us and hope to continue in life.

My third oldest brother also struggled, although he threw himself into sports and found success there. He, too, struggled in school; however, he made it through. He served in the Coast Guard and is definitely a survivor. Though he dished out many attacks towards me, I know that he was hurting, and my love for him remains; I choose love and forgiveness.

My oldest brother struggled the most. He felt abandoned and forsaken by our natural mother, which was understandable as he remembered her the most. He never understood why she never returned. Even though he was relieved when Dad showed up, my brother longed for her as any son would, and he had no control at his young age to change his circumstances. He did go to find her when he was an adult, and when he did, she rejected him again.

This left him devastated, and again, he would go off for periods of time trying to find his place in the world. My dad's anger clashed with his, and they were often at odds with one another. In an attempt to help him, many therapists were called in, and facilities were used to help stabilize him, but to no avail. They diagnosed him with bipolar disorder to try to define his struggle. However, I have always believed that he was sad and fought within himself against Dad's anger and our biological mom's rejection. In his travels, he would meet ladies, and his rage would fall on them. I still remember the face of one young lady and how bad she looked. My heart sank knowing that the rage was dripping from his sponge.

Our biological mom gave us all one thing: life. For this, we can all be grateful. However, her actions and consequences ripped at the shores of life with the path of destruction she had left. My father was broken, and now we are broken, too. While his intentions were in the right place, his actions often caused more trauma.

As we grew into adults, we took this brokenness with us. For me, I began to search for healing. I wanted to escape and get on with adult life and leave behind a childhood full of hurt. The weight of facing these struggles on a day-to-day basis became too heavy to bear, and I was ready to find freedom.

And not only so, but we glory in tribulations also:
knowing that tribulations worketh patience;
And patience, experience; and experience, hope:
And hope maketh not ashamed;
because the love of God is shed abroad in our hearts . . .

ROMANS 5:3-5

Hard is
Hard.
Hard is not
Bad.

Chapter 2

Freedom Isn't Free

The great thing about childhood is that it comes to an end. The hard thing is now we must think for ourselves. I wanted out of that house. I wanted to escape the day-to-day hardships that awaited me. I wanted independence and a way to set my own course. My heart was bleeding from the loss of my child, among many other events, and I needed help and support to find my way out. A fresh start where the challenges would not be so heavy. I needed love and affection that would give me the stability that I longed for. And I longed for it.

Well, God was at work again. An honorable man, Jeff, came into my life. A mutual friend set us up on a blind date. It was a unique date as he took me home to his parents' house for dinner. The reason is he had obtained custody of his almost one-year-old son, Daniel, at the time. The mother was mostly MIA (missing in action). As I sat on the couch meeting the whole family—mom, dad, two brothers, and a child—Daniel crawled up into my arms as if to say, "I choose you."

It was love at first sight. Not just for Jeff and me but also for Daniel and I. Daniel was the Band-Aid I needed for my bleeding heart. Jeff was the wound care I needed to feel loved and wanted. Though Jeff lived at home with the support of his family, they became an extension of my own family, and I loved how God's fingerprints were working on my life now.

Jeff's father also lost his dad at an early age. He was left to be the "man of the house" and took that role seriously. The family lived in New York, and once he became an adult, he joined the service and married Jeff's mother shortly after while in boot camp. Our stories blended the more we learned of each other and each other's families.

His parents were married twenty-four years when the divorce came. It was interesting to see that divorce affects adult children much like young children. All the children went through levels of anger and disgust. It took many years for relationships to mend, and Jeff's dad retreated to the mountains with his new wife, where they built a cabin.

Jeff's mom needed a lot of support, and as we attempted to care for her, she struggled to receive our help. Her heart was broken, and a lifetime commitment to her husband and children seemed to be tossed to the side with not much gratitude. Though she was trying to be independent, she found herself in several near-death experiences that we were able to pull her through; however, in her sixtieth year of life, her organs began to shut down, and we lost her to sepsis. Jeff's dad lived with his wife in their cabin until he lost his life to cancer. We were blessed to be present for both of their passings and repeat how much they were loved and how sad we were to see them go.

I remember the evening before his mother passed. I hung out at the hospital in the ICU, and we watched a movie. I don't know how aware she was that I was there; however, I acted as if it was just an evening watching a good Tom Hanks movie.

A little time hop backward: Jeff and I were married within three months of our blind date. Freedom had come. Or had it? We ended up living at his parent's house for a time before their divorce. I was now a wife and mother, and my little family was mine. I wanted to start a family right away. I wanted a child of my own, the right way.

While I was free from what I felt was a difficult situation, I was now bound to another. While living with Jeff's family, I experienced a whole different lifestyle. One of them is uncleanness and lack of care for the details of self-care or personal care. The children were held under the thumb of an angry dad with a drinking issue and a mother who had checked out because she couldn't cope with the life she was trapped in. While she tried to make the best of it, it was a heavy burden to bear.

Jeff always kept his space and Daniel's space very clean and organized. I was completely impressed. Jeff was on active duty in the military, so a whole new adventure began. I learned so much about what it meant to be a "single wife" and mother.

Even though I was ready to start a family right away, deployments would make getting pregnant very difficult, and it would be seven years until I was able to finally have a child of my own. I was desperate and fell to my knees and prayed as hard as I knew how for a child. Weeks later, I found out I was going to have a baby. Promise kept. Thirty-six weeks later, they laid Charles, named after his great-grandpa, grandpa, and uncle, in my arms; I was filled with love as I had never known before.

Military life was lonely, and there was a lot of isolation. I looked for ways to get out and become part of a community; however, it was hard. The trauma of childhood often bubbled up and was getting harder to keep compressed within my spirit.

I remember visiting with five other military wives as we were casually talking, and they were speaking very unkindly about their spouses aboard ship, and I just remained quiet. I knew the language of silence, and the outcome was very interesting because they heard me the loudest. My silence spoke volumes.

When asked why I was quiet, I could boast about my husband in a way that I didn't think they had ever heard before. Jeff had become the anchor I needed to hold life together, and there was nothing bad I could say about my situation or Jeff. That may have been a first. I believe that in that group of women, while I couldn't now tell you any of their names or what ship my husband was on that brought us all together, they had to reconsider all those negative comments and see their husbands in a new light.

I began to see how my brokenness could bring encouragement because I knew how other people were feeling. I spent my lonely hours going to school and preparing for a business career. When I completed my education and started working in business, I was able to see the customers' struggles and relate to their frustrations and quickly find solutions. This ability to work with customer-facing teams made me a favorite among upper management. Keeping the customers happy with minimal cost was beneficial to them, and I was able to communicate in ways that helped me gain favor not just with customers but with management. I was often asked for by name by my customers as they began to prefer to deal with me directly.

My professional life was going well; however, life on the inside spiritually was not. I found out that our son Charles would be the only child I would bear. I lost my balance, and the heaviness of life was weighing me down. The consequences of abortion caused problems that I was unaware of and prevented me from having any more children. Another loss, the feeling of failure, was brewing deep within. Freedom to have what I wished for was not free anymore. I was bound to a decision that I made for a lifetime. Years later, though successful in business, I found myself having to have the dreaded hysterectomy. Freedom from the home life I was escaping was still haunting me.

After the surgery, I met with my doctor for a follow-up, and she stated that the pathology report showed I shouldn't have even been able to carry Charles. God's handprint was on the very birth of my son. It has been stated to me on several occasions that he is a miracle baby, for which I am eternally grateful.

The years passed, and life seemed to balance out. The struggles of marriage and life seemed normal, and I was finding my way. The economy took a turn for the worse, and we hit rock bottom. Not knowing how to prepare or being prepared, we were caught in a trap. We ended up finding solace under the roof of my parents as they took us in to give us a roof over our heads.

Healing came and we were getting back on our feet. Due to my aging parents, we were asked to stay with them. It was different now. I was a mature, grown woman, not that little vulnerable girl anymore. I was able to confront the confusion by reminding my father that I was now a successful woman and could make decisions without his approval. It took some time for him to come on board with the mindset; however, once he did, our relationship began to heal. We spent hours together remembering stories and events from the past that we could now laugh over.

As we talked and I shared my views on life and solutions that I had created to deal with customers he was impressed and enjoyed listening to my mind at work. Perhaps he saw a little of himself in me as he, too, was a customer-first worker and could see that I had his heart for people.

My third oldest brother would come to visit while we lived with them, and he would often begin his verbal and emotional abuse. I reminded him, as well, that now I am an adult, and if it continued, I would take steps to ensure that it stopped. He heeded my warning, and the abuse stopped.

Jeff and I, along with our two sons, had moved into my parent's home and eventually began overseeing mostly house maintenance and smaller chores. My parents could still manage their meals and health conditions for a good many years into this arrangement.

Jeff felt the loss of no more children greater than I did, and he requested that we investigate foster care to see if it would be a good fit so that he could feel more children around and the parenting years he missed while in the military. We worked through the program to become foster parents. My parents agreed to our wishes and participated in the process as they were required. Three years in and six children later, our daughter, Selena, showed up at our door. She was tiny for her age, and as the details came out about her previous life, the trauma she had gone through touched my heart in a special way.

Unbeknownst to us at the time, she was born the same week as my dreaded hysterectomy. There was no way for me to know that as I was grieving a loss, God was making way for us to have a very special little girl who would need a mom like me who could understand her deepest feelings.

I knew how to communicate with her. I knew what she was feeling and how to guide and counsel her. Even though she didn't want to admit it, she felt safe and loved. She has often stated that she is thankful for a strict mother, which came from my upbringing. This is another example of my harsh childhood at work. I learned how to add grace to my trauma and now could use it to help others.

As I was working to connect with our daughter, the time came for me to say goodbye to my father. He was diagnosed with cancer with a short time to live. Having lived together by this time for about ten years, the healing of our relationship made it extremely difficult for us to say goodbye. I believe we both wished for more time in this stage of life, where we truly enjoyed each other and all the good memories we shared.

My favorite memory would be the time when he coached men's softball teams. I was his trained scorekeeper, and I could keep the scorebook under extremely distressed conditions. Other players would not wear uniforms, which made it hard to track them. My dad taught me how to track them, and many times, I could catch them batting out of order, costing the other team the game.

We were the perfect team, and I gained a reputation for catching details that other teams feared. Was this my hard childhood at work again? I knew how to maneuver through difficult situations and how important details mattered. This skill also spilled over into my professional world, and my attention to detail assisted me with my customers. I knew every detail about everything, and my quick mind and ability to find the solutions to indiscretions gave me the upper hand with accounts. My bosses would take notice of this, and I would be praised for my actions and for the accounts being so happy.

On one occasion, I had left one company and was taking some time off due to military life because kids and home needed my attention. Nana was ill and needed daily care, and we are firm believers that families should take care of their own.

I received a call from the business owner, and it was shared with me that the person who had taken my position had been stealing money from the business. As they were about to sell the business, they wanted me to come in and clean up the books so that the sale could move forward.

It was also shared with me that the customers still remembered me, and they were glad I was coming in to help. I found all the missing money and was able to support my findings and help the business complete its sale. The company that was purchasing them offered me a great position at a great salary, and I went back to work.

I may have been free from the constant influx of trauma from my childhood life, but it wasn't free. While the cost of all the trauma gave me skills that otherwise I may not have obtained, I was able to use my experiences to help others as I could identify the signs of when someone was in distress and needed support, or if they were the abuser, I knew how to keep them in their place. I was still easily triggered by the pain within, and finding that healing I longed for still seemed to elude me for a time.

As I continued to be successful in business, and God's hand stayed near me, I continued to pursue that deep happiness in my life. He sent us to a church with a pastor who spoke to my heart. I absorbed every part of what he was saying and dug into these mindsets, applying them to the hurt that dwelled within.

I learned my hardships were mine, and they were for a purpose. Knowing this, I was able to apply them, and the heavy spirit deep inside me began to lighten. The fingerprints of a higher power had not given up on me. Success starts with the desire to be more than you ever believed you could be. Dream bigger than you ever think you can, and set the bar high while never giving up.

And Jesus answered and said unto them,
Take heed that no man deceive you.

MATTHEW 24:4

Your
Response
Is
Your
Responsibility.

Chapter 3

Emotions

Our emotions are a critical part of the balance in our lives. They can be the helpers of life, like staff or workers, who take care of tasks for us so we can keep our households or businesses running efficiently. Emotions are the drivers of our outward responses. Our response is our responsibility. This includes how we respond when our emotions are triggered.

If we are easily triggered by what we carry and hide on the inside coming at us from what is happening on the outside from those we cannot control, we can lose the control we need for success. Customers and the public, in general, will spill whatever emotion they are feeling at the moment as it starts to overflow from the confines of within. Our reaction to them is critical. Knowing how to respond to that overflowing feeling of emotions and hurts will ensure that you can meet that customer where they are and help them to find their solution, which in turn helps to create a loyal customer by keeping our emotions balanced and under control.

People want to feel loved and valued. Don't you? We all want the chance at success, the opportunity to be given the chance to try to succeed. How those around us will receive us, whether it be in life or business, is out of our control. Not everyone is equipped to catch what is being dished out, and harm can and will be done. I believe I speak for many when I say it is uncomfortable and unwarranted.

However, if we can endure for a moment and see past the emotions spilling out, we can see the root of what is needed and bring them into our calm, helping them to find the resolution they are looking for. Knowing the different emotions and how to tame them gives us the ability to calm them and help the person know that we care and that we are here to help them find the resolution needed for success in the transaction, and we retain a loyal customer in each situation.

When we focus on all the faults and failures of life in general, it is easy to become unable to see or accept the truth of what is really happening within us or around us. We lose the focus needed by looking only at what is going wrong and not balancing it by seeing the success we are achieving or those that work for us.

Failure is a verb; it's motion. We do not fail until we quit. Quitting is where dreams go to die. Failure is one of the causes of the language of silence. We begin to withdraw and stop communicating. Digging into the cause causes more hurt and feelings, whether we are at fault or not. Time is the process that we use to let us find the right words to express our feelings safely and clearly.

We should always remind ourselves that it is okay not to be okay. We all mess up, and the freedom to mess up and learn is a great avenue for our feelings, worries, and fears. I love using the story of making bread with my teenage daughter. I wanted her to experience the patience of bread rising, the strength of your fingers to knead the dough, the smell of the yeast baking, and the taste of the warm bread with melted butter in her mouth.

It was an incredible amount of work and very easy to mess up, often needing several attempts, and wow, is it messy. The flour is everywhere in the space it takes to roll out the dough. It is everywhere. It is not always the journey we enjoy but the destination. It takes a lot to go on vacation, and I'm sure you can relate to needing a vacation from your vacation. Why? Because we exert so much effort to make it all perfect for the result, we often don't take into account what it takes to make it perfect. I'm sure we have all made mistakes in the processes of life; the great news is we get to try and try again. Don't be discouraged. It's okay. Don't quit; keep pushing through to the next experience, taking with you all the lessons you learn along the way.

Customer-facing teams and businesses are facing a huge gap in today's business world. Generations have lost face-to-face encounters and find it easier to only work within the world of computers and chats. Texting and chat tools remove the face-to-face altercations and the social interactions needed to deal with people on a day-to-day basis.

There are only six basic emotions. This theory of basic emotions and their expression, developed by Paul Ekman, dug into these emotions for a better understanding of their place in our lives.[2]

Sadness, enjoyment, fear, anger, surprise, and disgust make up the main emotions that we interact with on a day-to-day basis. We can find ways to control them in our lives appropriately, the key is to not let them linger in a negative way. Mixing some of these emotions together can go badly, like a science experiment going wrong.

Once, I got caught speeding on the highway. Fear immediately crept in. I wasn't sure what to expect, so I was truly afraid of the consequences, not only from the law but also from my husband. His displeasure with the cost of a speeding ticket made me more distressed than the ticket alone. His displeasure with me and my actions were more triggering to me as I wanted to be a good wife. I didn't want to cause him distress or the inconvenience of paying for a ticket.

Disappointment was not far behind. Grief topped this event like a cherry on an ice cream sundae. I knew I would receive a ticket, and I wanted to cry. When the situation was over, relief was not the dominant emotion. It took me some time to process through all these emotions, remind myself that I am not perfect, and make sure no one was expecting me to. It's not like my husband hasn't received any tickets, and I always gave grace, so why was I so worried about his reaction to me? Mostly it was because we are different and come from different backgrounds.

Enjoyment and happiness are most likely most people's favorite emotions. There was a time when I was having a hard day as Jeff was out to sea, and I was struggling with being that single mom. Our son Charles seemed aware of my distress, and he took a little Hershey's Kiss trinket box that played songs with the word "Kiss" in them. He placed a single chocolate kiss in the center, and as he called my name and I turned to see what his request was, he opened that box, and what a lovely surprise it was.

I felt loved and knew he understood my struggle in the moment and wanted to add joy to my world, even if just for a moment. I keep this trinket box stored in a tub of my favorite treasures. It no longer sings, but that memory lives in my heart all the days long.

Fear is the hardest emotion. There is a good fear and a bad fear. Bad fear can be defined as a sense of danger. Good fear is obeying or not breaking the law out of respect. Bad fear can be dangerous, and the cause and effect can be traumatic.

I was in a court waiting area due to our daughter's case regarding what happened to her while in the care of a certain couple before she came to be with us. The woman was very upset as her husband was the one being tried that day, and we were trying to settle the case without having to bring our daughter to court to face this person. Her voice continued to get louder and louder, and as they tried to calm her down, she only became more upset.

I took an opportunity to move over next to a police officer as I believed she knew who I was and why I was there. I was testifying in my daughter's place and accepting a plea agreement to keep her out of court. I explained to the court officer what was happening, and he remained with me until the process was over and I was escorted out of the building.

I used wisdom and understanding of fear to protect myself and make sure that no harm happened to me or anyone in the area. I believe the officer was grateful as well because he was informed of the potential danger and could ensure the situation didn't get out of hand.

Anger is a hard one to keep from bubbling out. The rage that anger triggers is hard to put out, like a fire out of control. This becomes the most challenging part of business with the hot customer. This is the customer that is already angry by the time you pick up the phone, and we are about to get a once-over for something we are not even responsible for.

I actually love the hot customers. The hotter, the better for me. While I know it's hard to be yelled at by anyone for a cause you may or may not be responsible for, the amount of information coming out of that customer tells a story. If we can hear the details through the storm and bring that storm into our calm, we can achieve an amazing solution for our customers. This gives us the best opportunity to create a loyal customer, and we will become their favorite agent due to the fact that we kept our calm and ended the hardship they had. It is actually a wonderful feeling for me.

Disgust can be kind of fun. It depends on the situation. I don't want to dig through trash looking for something. Yuck! Disgust can come at us without warning, and we get to just deal with it. We were on a road trip for the day, and it was a rough trip. Remember that speeding ticket. Whew, many emotions going on there.

We decided to just go to a restaurant for dinner and decompress. Easy enough. Well, the waitress came to the table with the complementary water, and the glass tipped over and ran down the leather booth I was sitting on. The waitress was clearly sorry, as it was not on purpose, and I was not upset. I saw that it was a mistake and that life happens. Just not the best day to have happened on.

She immediately stated that she would get the manager, and I replied that I just needed a towel. Many onlookers were watching, and I wanted to show the best parts of me. They were able to see that I took on the challenge with grace and peace, and we cleaned it all up and ordered our meal.

The manager came over, and we explained that we were fine and wanted nothing to happen to the waitress. Yes, I was disgusted. I was wet, cold, and frustrated. However, I would not let any of that bubble out and displayed the me I wanted to be in that moment.

Meet surprise. Surprise is like a two-edged sword. On the one hand, a dozen roses from Jeff's sweet gesture to show his love for me and my love for flowers is pleasant. On the other hand, an unmet expectation causes extreme disappointment to the receiving person.

Like when I was eight years old and shook every apple off the tree. I was expecting my dad to be proud of me. I mean, he commented the previous day that he didn't know how he would get the apples from the top of the tree down. However, I was unaware that all the apples were hitting the ground as I looked up, shaking the branches. Not understanding how that number of apples would impact my parents, I felt that I was being helpful.

I still remember the dozens of brown paper bags full of apples covering the floor of the back room of the house. My mom was loyal from a distance on the sidewalk while my dad went door to door, repeating the story. God bless her. I have no memory of picking up a single apple or the door-to-door journey. I'm sure I have blocked that out due to extreme distress.

While this memory is funny today, it was not on that day. On that day, I was completely surprised to find out that my dad was not as excited as I was. I learned a valuable lesson that day on quantity versus quality. It has always been a reminder to look through the lens of a person's actions before I go to judge them. Their heart may have been in the right place, but the actions needed some understanding.

Extra Emotions

In addition to the six most experienced emotions, there are a few more that I would like to introduce you to. Disappointment is yet another emotion that can be life-changing. In the King James Version of the Bible, the word "disappointment" doesn't exist. God never mentions that he is disappointed with us. Why? Disappointment in reverse is expectations unmet. Why were we expecting that? If we acknowledge God is the highest power in the land and is never disappointed with us, then why would we ever be disappointed? This is life-changing. If we can live in the mindset of not having an expectation of anyone, then disappointment should not exist.

When our customers call upset because they had an expectation of goods or services we did not meet, then we must find the root cause and correct it. What did we communicate that would give them that expectation? I believe we could never have another disappointed customer again. If we ensure that we know their expectations and verify that they truly understand, we will only have satisfied customers.

While humility has some characteristics of an attitude, it is also an emotion that we should harness and incorporate into our character. Not so much as an attitude to dealing with customers, but with a soft sense of attention to their needs in finding a solution to their problem. We should come in soft and with an open mind to listen and respond appropriately, preserving the customer relationship and gaining loyalty.

Many feelings are rooted in emotions. Taking time to learn and understand how to master them will always be beneficial to all involved.

Wisdom is the principal thing; therefore get wisdom: and with all thy getting get understanding.

PROVERBS 4:7

Chapter 4

_____

Knickknacks On The Shelf

I love displaying all my favorite treasures in my home. My favorite books line up the rows of my bookshelves. The handprint of my son painted so terribly. The "I Love Mom" woodworking craft from my oldest son. I get to see it every time I wash the dishes, as it is above the molding of the window by the sink. My refrigerator, covered in pictures, is the museum my kids display so I can see their priceless works of art.

Professional pictures and snapshots of moments in time that I want to hold onto are on that refrigerator. It is amazing how much we spend on businesses to display all these treasures. Everyone has a particular way of doing so, from clean and organized to the "Just throw it on the shelf." style. I am clean lines and organized.

While I enjoy the display of my knickknacks on my shelves, there is another shelf we must acknowledge. This is the shelf on the inside where we hide all the parts of life that didn't go well. The ex-partner, the miscarriage of the child we longed for, the traumas of hurt and bleeding wounds that no one sees. What shelf are they on? We may not see them on a regular basis; however, we "feel" them—that deep ache within trying to get out all the while we continue to push them down.

I recall a time while visiting a friend, and I was shocked to see a side of them that I had never seen before. It was near the holidays, and they received a phone call from another family member who challenged the calendar and made some birthday plans for their child difficult to accommodate. Even though they were three rooms away, the sound was so loud that we could hear every word. We became very uncomfortable with the situation, so we just went to bed for the night.

The next morning, they were still steaming, and all the information was pouring out. They were still clearly upset, feeling as if their request was not respected. Their child's birthday was forsaken for something that didn't matter in their opinion that much. I later learned that the family member they had berated so badly ended up in a divorce. While I do not believe it was from that one event, I imagine that their siblings were already in distress trying to keep peace within the family during the holiday season and didn't need any more negativity. I learned that once that conversation was over with the one family member, they called another family member to vent. All of this was being witnessed by their children.

I was very disheartened at this event and began to fear that my friend, whom I truly respect and often sought counsel from, would react like that to me someday. I began to walk on eggshells, never knowing if what I was saying or doing would trigger whatever emotion was on the inside to come spewing out. Friendships come and go, and it was clear that I needed to put some distance between us out of protection for myself and for them, as I would never want to provoke them to react in such a manner. I still love my friend dearly; however, we are not as close as we used to be or even could be.

Hurt affects us all. We may be able to hide these effects. Nonetheless, the jolt to our emotions is clear. We are all capable of triggering someone unaware of what is on the inside from past experiences. We always risk the possibility of stinging their trauma without warning, and if they have not processed through these hurts, then they are easily triggered.

When we look beyond all the hurts, disappointments, and pains that challenge us and expose our core, we can cut the taproot that has taken hold of us. When eradicating poison ivy, you must cut it at the base. This cuts off all the nutrition to the outer plant, and it dies. Ivy grows like a cactus. The roots below the surface can go for miles looking for water. That is why you can see one green cactus in the middle of a desert, just as happy as it can be. This is why poison ivy can pop up anywhere, anytime, just like the emotions we have buried on those shelves inside.

These emotions take hold of us like an electrocution. As a younger inexperienced lady, I was cleaning out my car. I decided to use Nana's old Electrolux vacuum cleaner. The problem was that the ground was wet, and the plug was not grounded due to the age of the vacuum. Barefoot, I picked up that metal tube, which grabbed me with a jolt of electricity that I could not let go of. It had grabbed me, and no matter how much I wanted to let go, I could not.

Balance

All these emotions that we have on our internal shelves need balance. Take time to process them and ensure they are not gripping us and that the roots are cut back and not controlling our behaviors and interactions with others.

When we have this balance, we take their power over us away. While all life experiences are part of our journey in life, they are also meant for us to grow and mature into the individuals we want to be.

Focus on what you know, not what you feel. Emotions react to how we feel, leaving feelings to dictate our emotions. Leaving these feelings aside and going with what you know takes the power of emotions away and helps us to become more centered on what is.

Not dealing with the feelings that are feeding our emotions can lead to health issues, along with substance abuse, homelessness, incarceration, poor quality of life, unemployment, or worse, suicidal ideations.[3]

The U.S. Centers for Disease Control and Prevention reports that heart disease, cancer, and diabetes are among the leading causes of death and disability in the United States.[4] These diseases affect not only the individual holding onto emotions but also the country, costing over four trillion dollars in annual health care costs.

The British Journal of Psychiatry reported on a total population study that showed an increased mortality rate among those diagnosed with anxiety disorders. Their results showed that 2.1 percent with anxiety disorders died during an average follow-up of 9.7 years. The risk of death by natural and unnatural causes was significantly higher. Of those who died from unnatural causes, 16.5 percent had been diagnosed with depression. The conclusion was that these disorders played an important part in the increased mortality.[5]

In business, this comes at us from both sides of the counter. How to balance out what is in our companies and what is coming from our customers is a delicate balance.

There is this old story that stuck in my mind about a worker whose job was to take one boulder to the top of the hill using a wheelbarrow. Seems easy enough. However, on his way up the hill, other workers noticed the wheelbarrow and asked if they could put their boulder in while he was on his way up. The worker obliged and allowed the others to place theirs in the wheelbarrow. The problem was the wheelbarrow had become too heavy, and he was no longer able to push it up the hill.

He took on more than required, and he couldn't do his job. We do this in life. We pick up others' emotions because we can relate or we have compassion to help. Then, in time, the weight begins to be too much for us to carry our own emotions and the emotions of others.

Being mindful of the amount we are carrying and choosing only to carry that which we are able to process and assist with keeps us balanced and still able to help those we wish to.

I attended an event many years ago, and it was shared that we worry about events that will never occur. I wrote the details in the margin so I would not forget them. While I am sure the stats have changed over the years, here is what is in the margin of that book.

Forty percent of events we worry about will never happen; 30 percent of them are in the past and cannot be changed; 12 percent is simply criticism of others; 10 percent is regarding health; and only 8 percent are real problems we will face.[6]

Keeping emotions centered and remaining in the mindset of reality, that 8 percent is a critical practice so we stay balanced and decrease the risk of expediting something that will never come to pass.

Emotional scars and healing are an important part of self-care. Setting aside time to process and research why you might feel the way you do empowers you with the wisdom you need to find the healing and balance of what you feel.

Being ready to meet the day, knowing that you are as balanced as possible within, will lead to success in your personal life, professional life, and spirit within. Being happy with the person you are or want to be brings about success for us. We choose what we consider to be success in our lives. Having the balance on the inside and on the outside brings peace and strength to continue pursuing what we dream of.

The healing emotions from my internal shelf regarding my dad came when I pulled off all the band-aids of life and let the real wounds show. Often, wounds need to heal from the inside out. If we close them up, they only get worse underneath the bandages. If we don't apply healing medication, then the wound continues to grow and get worse.

It still took years; however, once my dad saw my success and the tools he had taught me through the years stuck with me, he began to let me be the woman I was supposed to be. A few weeks before he passed, as we were talking, he gave me a charge to care for my mom.

It was so hard on him knowing he was going to be leaving us, and as I cared for him alongside my mother until his passing, I was able to let go of the many wounds and pour over them the forgiveness he so longed for.

After being up all night, I told him I was going to go rest for a bit, and I would be back soon. The last words he ever spoke were to me. "See you later, baby girl." This memory is safely stored on the internal shelf close to my heart. For all the hard days, his last words were for me. I cherish this memory, and if I could put it in a picture, it would be displayed on my wall.

The years have passed since his passing, and life has been very different. I am left with the charge of caring for Mom, which I take great honor in fulfilling. I am truly thankful that he is at rest from all the hurts of the past, that he is reunited with two of his sons who awaited him on the other side, and that he has no more pain or rage to fight for that which life dished out so willingly.

I am at peace with my emotions and can conquer the days ahead with a clear mind and an open heart. Yes, I still take time to grieve, mourn, or whatever I am feeling. I keep my knickknacks inside in order and have a great understanding of their roots and how to maintain them by the understanding of what put them there and that 8 percent of how they will actually affect me.

A Special Gift

I am not known as a pet person. I will take a pet rock and have a few. As a little girl, we had twenty-six cats and kittens at one time. While I loved and cared for these animals, owning and caring for animals is low on my list. My love of caring for people has grown to where I intend to be the best there is. My bar is set pretty high, but it's mine.

However, I am married to a dog man. I always joked that one day, if I had a dog, a dog that was my own, I would want a boy and name him Dude. Well, it happened. He came at the exact time I needed him. Dude came a few months after my dad passed, which hit me hard.

In my dad's last days, I was able to thank him for all the sacrifices that he made for all of us. He often recalled and apologized for how hard he was on us, and as he did, we reminded him that we forgave him for all that; he was the best dad, and we would miss him very much when his time came. He didn't care to talk about the day that he would leave us; however, I always reminded him every day that I loved him and appreciated all that he had done to protect us from what we didn't know.

Dude somehow knew that I was struggling when no one else really did. He reminded me of my dad. While I don't believe in reincarnation, if my dad were to have come back as a dog, it would have been Dude. He never leaves my side, and he "protects" me from my own husband—he will not allow my husband or children to sit next to me. He always sleeps with me and steals all my blankets. Dude shares the birth date with my oldest brother, and he was a dude too. This didn't occur to me at first, so it's ironic how it all worked out.

So, while I am not a pet person, I will always be a Dude person. He is the perfect companion for me and gives me love and comfort in the place where loneliness dwells. He chooses to be where I am and comforts me when I need comfort. No matter who is calling him away from me, he always stays by my side.

He helps my emotions on hard days and days when I am reminded of the losses that life revealed; he knows. He crawls up on my chest, lays his head on my shoulder, and stays for as long as I need him to. I don't call him to do this task; he already knows. If he can't sit on my chest for whatever reason, he sits by or near me.

When I'm at my desk, he crawls in my bed and watches from afar. If I move, he looks up to survey my movements. If I leave the room, so does he. He is a very good dog and always obeys my commands. I love it when members of my family try to call him away from me. Even with my encouragement to comfort them, he simply sits with me. He is very chill and goes with the flow.

He loves to be held but, of course, only by me. If I am outside walking around, he will come up and try to jump in my arms. I will pick him up like a little two-year-old, and he will just perch in my arms until it is time to head to the next task. I often say he would let me hold him all day.

I love the comfort he brings and dread the day I will have to say goodbye to him. He is the main knickknack on my shelf inside my heart. My family knows exactly what is to be done if, for some reason, I pass before him, as he is to be given the same afforded as he is used to by me. He is never in trouble and never causes any disruptions—that is unless you threaten me.

Angie and Dude

Peace I leave with you, my peace I give unto you:
not as the world giveth, give I unto you.
Let not your heart be troubled, neither let it be afraid.

JOHN 14:27

Don't ruin
a good
apology
with an
excuse.

Chapter 5

The Cycle Of A Relationship

Graphic created by Ms. Angie

First, we love them, then we judge them, and sometimes we forgive them. This cycle of a relationship, though short, leaves a long-lasting effect. Our first teachers in life are our parents, and their brokenness, even though they may try their best, rubs off on us. Trauma drips like that soaked sponge. Unfortunately for children, the damage can be done before the consequences are ever discovered. Children don't know how to handle their emotions, and some people are triggered by even hearing about trauma as it brings them back to their own. Staff that has not practiced this cycle will struggle on both sides of the counter. Fixing our brokenness starts by acknowledging it.

It is so important in relationships to understand that we are all not perfect and have a mindset to accept that we all mess up. This struggle for some comes from a wide range of reasons, from trauma to shame, and taking steps to be humble and having the courage and willingness to accept the actions and consequences will help us grow and stay successful.

Those who struggle with taking accountability will display certain traits such as avoidance, procrastination, accepting criticism, over-reliance on others, lack of self-awareness, and a few others.[7]

Integrity is a great character trait to possess. Doing what you say you will do no matter if the circumstances change or become worse. Imagine everything going wrong in an instant. Would you carry out what you said you would do, or would you bail?

We should also address the correlation between emotions and personalities. Researchers believe in an intricate connection between personality and emotions. In simple terms, "personality refers to enduring characteristics and unique adjustments to life, including major traits, interests, drives, and values, along with thinking and feeling patterns and characteristics of a person shaped by an intricate interplay of nature and nurture."[8] Emotions are patterns of behavioral and physiological reactions to specific events with variations and maladaptive forms.[9]

Research is important to know what it takes to achieve the goals we have set for ourselves. Our bar is ours to set. We cannot set someone else's bar, and they cannot set ours. Equally, we don't hold someone else responsible for reaching our goals as we are not required to reach theirs.

Setting the bar of success affects our livelihoods, our families, our careers, and our balance within ourselves. I love people, all people, and I love tending and nurturing them and their needs if I am able. I love to hear all the stories as I get to know them better and develop relationships.

Setting The Bar

Where do you want your bar to be? What is the plan to get there? The power is within each one of us to know our limitations and the ability to dream beyond them. We find success when we choose to be the people we want to be and follow those ambitions.

Now, this road is not for the faint at heart; it takes dedication and grit. Never giving up on ourselves or our dreams takes balance and determination. And while I never like to push religion, a little bit of praying never hurts.

In my balance of life, there has always been a part of spirituality that keeps me feeling whole. I know this is not for everyone; however, in the cycle of relationships, I lift people up all the time who don't even know it, and I get to sit by and watch the potter work.

It's messy in the front row, but it is the best seat in the house. As we watched our daughter transform into this amazing lady, we went through the battle of a lifetime. Having to unlearn all the behaviors that were causing harm and retraining her to be the successful lady she is today has been a transformation that could only be a miracle.

It is unfortunate that many businesses are currently having to take on a larger role in training staff and management. The demands of technology place us in a different environment, not only in the office but in the world. Businesses must be ready to meet each customer where they are and the needs that they are looking for quickly and efficiently without failure.

Customers are now leaving businesses after only one bad experience because of the disconnect between the customer and the business. In a survey of two thousand, one in six abandoned their purchase over one bad experience. Even loyal customers, after only a few bad experiences, will leave the company in search of better service.[10]

Understanding this cycle and training our staff to understand its value benefits our companies by maintaining long-lasting relationships with our staff and customers for years to come.

We may only see the victory, not realizing all the work it takes to arrive. Victory can be a long road in a short life. Working diligently while never letting our guard down or giving up on ourselves leads to success for ourselves and for our businesses. When we reach the mark we set for ourselves, we obtain what we hoped for.

C.A.R.E.
Customers Are Relationship Equity

Preparing a customer service team means we are giving them the tools they need to be successful. When we empower people who serve us with the tools that they need to be able to relate to potential clients and one another, we are creating an environment for success. Team members must understand what it means to have that face time with a customer, even if it is just over the phone.

- **Customers**: individuals who voluntarily choose what business or corporation they will purchase products or services from
- **Are**: every person, pet, or plant owner that at some point will need services and goods. It is only a matter of who will

receive their business. Even the individual who owns the business is a customer to someone.

- **Relationship**: the way two or more people bridge a process or contract for the benefit of each other in the purchase of goods or obtaining services.
- **Equity**: the value of the transaction. Money is the main bridge between every customer and every transaction, not just for one transaction but also for the long-term investment that you make in the individual or business.

The relationship with a customer is key in all business. Customers want a meaningful relationship with the people they are doing business with. Even the place we go for gas for our cars is important. We want someone reliable and pleasant for services and goods, so much so that we are willing to pay more for the services and goods. Statistics show that customers will pay more for services and goods if the customer service meets their expectations.[11]

Stand out. Find ways to up your game to make sure that you are reaching your community and industry. Be the name that people want to talk about positively in their circles. Being dependable and ready to serve is attractive to everyone looking on.

Valuing complaints not as feedback but as "feedforward" gives space for growth for employees and customers. Saying "thank you," as opposed to "I'm sorry," communicates to the customer that you appreciate and value their input.

Another statistic shows that consumers are not likely to call in to report failures. They simply move on, and a customer is lost without the business knowing it. So, if a dissatisfied customer takes the time out of their day to report insights into failures within our businesses, then "thank you" is appropriate.[12]

A brother offended is harder to be won than a strong city: and their contentions are like the bars of a castle.

PROVERBS 18:19

Chapter 6

Five Degrees Of A Customer

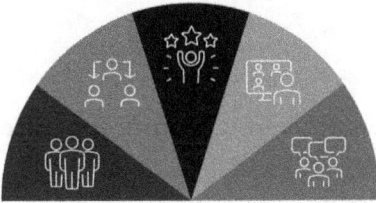

Graphic created by Ms. Angie

Are you familiar with the seesaw? The piece of playground equipment where two parties go up and down on a long board, often metal, balancing on a single support in the middle. It only works when there are two parties, and the simple motion of going up and down brought enjoyment to those talking and laughing while gravity did its job.

The five degrees of a customer are a lot like that seesaw. Balance is key. Until now, we have been discussing balance as the main point of success. Understanding the balance within will benefit us from the balance on the outside when dealing with all types of customers.

Who are these customers? We may have some preconceived ideas about who they are; however, if we look at the true definition of a customer, we find that it is everyone we meet. As we dive into this mindset, let's start with the definition of what a customer is:

- A person or organization that buys goods or services
- A person or a thing of a specified kind (as we will see below) that one has to deal with.

As we break down each degree, the hope is you will take a moment to consider who might be in each degree in your personal world.

Degree One

Degree one customers are those who are in your space. The people, pets, and plants that you live with in your home. They dwell among you and rely on you in some ways for survival. While people can help participate in their lives, you are their companions, overseers, and, in some cases, care providers. Pets cannot get a job to support their needs for food, medical, etc. They can't go to the store to purchase their necessities—they are not even able to fill their water or food bowls. Yet they give so much to us as companions and comfort. We often have a need to care for a life totally dependent on us, and pets meet that need.

Plants. I love my plants. I prefer outdoor plants as they require less direct care from me; however, I do have one in the home from a memory from Grandma Rose. I assure you that if I do not water it, prune it, and give it the nutrients it needs, it will die.

The importance of degree one is that it should be balanced out with the weight of degree five for the seesaw to function at its best; the weight distribution should be as close as possible.

Degree Two

Degree two makes up the extended family, friends, and community that you socialize with. While these individuals do not have direct demands for you on an ongoing basis, we spend a good amount of time with them, thinking of them and, in some cases, supporting them in their endeavors.

This is also the degree to which many friends enter and exit our lives as I learned as a military spouse. Some friends are only meant to stay for a season. While long-distance friendships can be special, they are rare, as time and space tend to drift people apart.

They do add value to your business and career. They often know you best and see what you don't. Their input will be honest and raw; though you may not see it that way, it is important to have their insights for growth and pruning. Like our plants, they grow best when they are pruned correctly.

Staying on our toes and continuing to provide the best of ourselves to all those around us leaves a long-lasting impression that will continue to ripple like the smooth pond the rock was tossed into. Having a heart for service to everyone you meet, without judgment, will make an impact that will leave you with a legacy of success you can be proud of.

Degree Three

This is the degree for us. I love the mindset that self-care is not first care. There has never been a time in my life when I could choose me first. I have always balanced out my needs with those of the other degrees.

It is important to see yourself as a customer and with you, the customer, being served by another business or service provider. It is important to make sure that we are good customers on both sides of the counters. What I mean by both sides of the counter is that when we are serving and when we are being served should match.

We will have moments where we fall short, and so will other businesses. We should always extend the grace we wish to receive. I have a hamburger place that we visit frequently when life gets busy. The hard part is pickles. Yes, pickles. I always ask them to hold the pickle, yet I am always picking pickles off my sandwich.

I could go in and request them to make it again. However, I choose not to. I know that they receive a lot of criticism already from a lot of other sources, and I want to be a good customer. So, I keep picking off the pickles.

They know us well, and we are always greeted well and have a great experience with the people. That is way more important to us than pickles. I treat my own customers this way. I focus on them, then the details of the service. While I verify the information, I am on a higher level of business than a sandwich, and I have more at stake.

In business, I always want to know the two steps ahead of me and the two steps after me. I want to be the safety net for my company and my team. If I know the steps ahead, then I can identify what was missed, and if I know the steps after me, I can prepare my customers for success when handing them to the next person with all the information required.

Like the seesaw, I am the center point. The balance for both sides is going up and down, and I want them to have a smooth ride. Remember that the seesaw was meant for enjoyment with a friend. So, maintaining that spirit, I position every encounter to be successful and enjoyable.

Degree Four

We have arrived at work. This is where we will spend most of our time away from home. Where we build our careers, hopes, and dreams for our future successes. Where you can build a reputation for taking care of and serving others well; for some, it is getting the education needed to build on other successes or be the launching place for those first steps.

We always paid our kids for their grades as we viewed school as their job. Their job was to do well and get a good education for their future. They never failed to turn in their grades to receive compensation, which was a great motivator for them to be vigilant in their studies.

Once we take that first step on the ladder of employment, we never want to take it lightly. I want to know how high this ladder goes, what steps I need to take to reach the top. This is important in business because some businesses do not have the structure to carry us very far. It is okay if it does not; the experience can be worth the time spent.

The "hot" customers are angry and spewing out frustration like a tornado. These happen to be my favorite customers. Like a tornado hunter, I love being in the eye of the storm, grabbing all the details while getting to the solution quickly.

While I know it is not for everyone, I don't mind verbal abuse or the cause of why they are upset. What can they do to me? I don't take it personally. Many upset people only spill out what is on the inside, and I am just in the path. If I can bring peace to their world, even for a moment in time, I want to be that person.

Communication is key when speaking with any customer. Often, miscommunication is what causes the problem. Either someone didn't make it clear, or they had a preconceived idea that was not correct.

We can tell them they are wrong, however, we will only make it worse, and there is no profit in telling them they are at fault. It is always wise to walk them through the process and empower them to have a complete understanding of the process to bring them closer to what expectations they should have; meaning disappointment will cease to exist.

I want to take this opportunity to remind you that the words "thank you" are appropriate here. Only one in nine will call to tell us something is wrong, so admitting failure is not beneficial until you are fully aware that failure occurred.[13] So, the upfront response is to thank them for making us aware and then digging into the details.

Employees change jobs on an average of every 2.73 years.[14] Experience is key to success, and learning different styles and standards will assist us as we climb the ladder. Never stop advancing and looking for the next experience.

This also helps us to stay on our toes, to make sure our skills are sharp, and we stay ready to serve where we are needed and wanted. Always creating relationships with many industries and businesses gives us the best opportunities to have many options as we find the ones we want.

Degree Five

Once again, keeping in mind the balance of the seesaw, we must use degree one and five as counterweights. We want the ride to be smooth and fun; therefore, giving attention to both equally is imperative, and I always pay attention to these details.

Degree five is the customers you attract. This is where your light shines, and all the best parts of us should be visible. These customers can come to us by referral or reputation, and they may even be customers we have never met before.

In high school, I was tasked to sell eight boxes of doughnuts to cover my Future Homemakers of America Club dues. I went on a quest and ended up selling two-hundred and ninety-eight boxes of doughnuts. I learned that I had the ability to connect with people, and they would buy my product. It was not necessarily the doughnuts they were buying; they could do that without me. It was me that brought them joy and a willingness to purchase what I was selling.

Not only did I meet the requirements for my dues, but the doughnut shop also offered me a job. At the young age of seventeen, I worked several evenings a week and weekends caring for their customers, and I learned how to make doughnuts. It was a great experience at a young age, and I looked forward to interacting with the customers.

Sometimes, careers pick us. Our strengths become the guiding tools that direct our path in life and career. No skill comes at birth. In our first twenty-four hours, we learn to cry, breathe, and eat—a busy day.

Making that first impression is beyond amazing—building the bridges that support the relationship with conversations that help us get to know our future customers on a more personal level. One thing I have learned for sure is people love to talk about themselves.

Drama Drama Drama

There is drama in customer service, suspense about what will happen next, and never knowing exactly what is on the other side of the counter/phone, from a love scene to a traumatic killing. The secret is how to respond quickly and appropriately. This eludes many businesses and customer-facing teams.

Selling is not the hardest part of customer success that would lead the customer to choose your business to serve them.

In today's generation, gaps in knowledge and technological advancements have made it challenging for businesses to stay staffed. Many customer-facing teams are losing the face-to-face skills needed to interact with the public.

The good news is that now that we have so many new options to interact with customers, having all of them available helps us stand out. From texting to chats and face-to-face, it adds the ability to reach more customers. Having the staff to meet each direction is key.

Some customers still want to talk to a person; some just want to chat. Communication on all levels is critical as they use different aspects.

Intention and interpretation do not always walk the same road. We can chat with the best intentions, but we cannot control the interpretation—it is more difficult to verify orders and requests. Verbal and written communication are different, and while both are important, knowing the difference is key to a successful transaction.

Money revolves around every transaction. Whether it be money in or money out. Money is also a very volatile topic. The balance of monies in and monies out for both the customer and the business also requires balance. It is up to the staff to understand the equity of each customer and balance that out with the needs of the company.

But he, being full of compassion,
forgave their iniquity, and destroyed them not:
yea, many a time turned he his anger aways,
and did not stir up all this wrath.
For he remembered that they were but flesh;
a wind that passeth away,
and cometh not again.

PSALM 78:38-39

Experience is
taught through
action,
not through
words.

Chapter 7

Success Starts With You

When individuals want to get into shape or learn to lift weights, they are all recommended to start off small. Walk a small amount and build on it little by little to build up stamina. When lifting weights, we start with a small amount of weight with the same number of repetitions. It is the addition of weight while continuing the repetitions that help gain strength. Simple increases over time build strength in any area, whether it be physical or emotional. The value and importance of this progress is key to growing in all areas of life.

I call my first son the "test baby" as he taught me through my many mistakes, and by the time I was on to my third child, I was more or less a "professional." Not really; there is always room for growth or gaining more knowledge and education, from small life responsibilities to the care of corporations.

Building success means we build on our little success as we grow. In this case, going from lifting five pounds to fifty pounds is a success. All levels of increased ability equal success. Experience is the best growth for personal, professional, and spiritual growth.

Breaking these down into independent quests allows us to deal with each section before blending all of them together for the balance we need overall. First, we must decide on what field, position, or industry we want success in. For me, I love people, and I love serving people. It is my heart's craft to master and perfect. I love their stories and experiences, and what I can take away from their experiences and apply them to my life is such a benefit to me, even if they don't realize it. No matter what journey we decide on, people are the common denominator. Knowing how to maneuver through different kinds of people is critical to all success.

It requires a lot of experience and knowledge about a large group of people. For example, the multi-cultural population. This means understanding cultures and traditions is important to understanding why people do what they do. While it is a big task, there are a lot of similarities that help manage this group. Keeping boundaries personally, professionally, and spiritually assists us in whatever situation we may find ourselves in.

Recapping situations we have encountered and replaying them with different outcomes can prepare us for our reactions on different levels. This equips us to use one situation and use it on several different levels. I always refer to the onion. There are lots of layers, and they all have relevance. I have a little notepad I carry with me where I jot down the examples I want to process more and analyze different avenues where the situation could have gone.

Living in the scenario of "what if" can be productive. It allows us to come up with solutions that can be used at different times and in different situations. There is no one cookie cutter solution for every event. By processing the events in our path, we empower ourselves to grow and research new and more effective ways of interacting with the population for the success of ourselves and our businesses.

Personally

When we start off in childhood, it is through play we learn how to treat others through direction from our parents, even our toys. We learn to treat them with value and respect as they become our first friends. Little girls often use baby dolls to impersonate their children and families. Through this play, we see the hearts of children and what their expectations may be.

When our foster daughter first came, she was playing with the dolls we had. She slapped the doll across the face. Now, understanding that she did not come from an environment where she was nurtured and taught, we stepped in and gently talked about her reasons and ours and why we do not treat the babies this way. It was a great teaching moment.

These are our first "what if" moments in life as they tap into our desires to create and invent the life that we dream of. I believe many struggle with the age difference. We are not little children anymore; however, as adults, we still have a desire to create and invent what we dreamed of.

I wish and hope for that chance to have the opportunity to succeed. Wanting someone to take a chance on us will open the door for us to show what we have created or invented to have our success personally. Often, it seems extremely discouraging when looking for that job when we have no real on-the-job experience. We ask, how are we to get experience if no one is willing to give us any? Many employees are looking for that, but obtaining it is challenging. Even coming fresh out of college with a degree can be challenging to find the "dream" job.

As we begin pursuing what our dream career will be, we are looking for that opportunity to come in our direction. Being at the right time at the right place with the correct tools in hand is how we stand out.

A lifetime prison sentence is measured in twenty year increments. These are where the small weights come in, so by the time we are in our twenties, the ambitions and dreams that we want should be on our horizons. However, if we didn't prepare to meet this challenge in time, we run late. Preparing as soon as possible puts us at the best advantage for success.

Once, there was an old building with an older elevator. When it broke down, there was only one person to call. He knew the elevator well because of his experience with it and could diagnose the problem quickly. The company was getting behind as the elevator moved the product from one floor to the other, and they desperately needed the elevator to keep up with the demands.

The repair man fixed it quickly and then handed the owner a bill for ten thousand dollars. The owner, distraught over the cost, asked how it could be so much; it was only a screw that you replaced. The repair man simply replied, well, it is only a dollar for the screw; knowing where to put the screw is nine thousand nine hundred and ninety-nine dollars.

The repair man knew his value because he knew what needed to be done. This often happens in life. The solution is easy; knowing the solution creates our value. However, it leaves the owner at the mercy of the bill.

The deep desire to be valuable starts with our specialties. What do we really want to be when we grow up? What do I want to spend my lifetime accomplishing? If we don't like teeth, we probably shouldn't be a dentist.

If you're not a people person, then working directly with the public will be more challenging for you. Some get along with everyone and just connect quickly with many personalities and individuals. Finding out where we fit best and building on that drives us to success.

I have had several careers that I have experienced on my journey. I wanted to try a little bit of everything. I have learned a great number of different avenues that are useful to me across the board.

Imagine spending thousands of dollars on schooling for your future, whether trade school or college. You graduate with a degree and get a job unrelated to your degree, but when you arrive at the job, nothing seems familiar. I know many who go to school for one major and never end up working in that major.

I have been in this situation with the schools that I attended. Once I graduated and found a job, the job was nothing like the degree I received. So, what expectations did we put on our education? What expectations should we have put on our education? Before expecting anything from higher education, which I believe is important, we should research what is required for that role. Researching what it takes to achieve what you determined would be your purpose empowers you to have a complete understanding of what needs to be prepared. I didn't know that I should do any research at the time, so I arrived at the job unprepared.

We depended on the school to tell us what we needed; now, while they may have an order or system they used to come up with those details, we should verify them as well. Falling onto the advice that someone else gives sets us up for disappointment. In the end, their recommendations can fail, and the result is you still get the bill. We trusted their advice, and while trust is important, always, and I do mean always, doing our own homework will ensure that the direction we are heading is the way we want to go.

My husband and I were on a road trip early in our marriage. I oversaw the map, which was a bad idea. The entire time, I knew we would be heading west and north. The problem was on the way home; my mind was still focused on north and west, and that is the way we continued. After about a hundred miles, I realized that we should be going south and east, as I saw the sign saying how many miles to go to California. We lived on the East Coast. It is a fun memory for us during our early years together. However, I am not sure how much he trusts me with direction anymore.

Success is walking in, ready to go. If we are as prepared as possible, we will need minimum training, which will benefit the business. One business I had been hired at was part of the medical industry, and I was hired to cover the front desk where the phones were. I was the first face of the customers, both at the door and on the phone.

They were expecting me to be ready in two weeks to answer the phone, but what they didn't know was that I was already trained. I only needed a few facts, and I was ready. My boss was thrilled that on day three, I answered the phones and transferred calls, all the while tending to customers who were walking in. It may have been such a relief for her as they were struggling in this department, and my training was what they had been hoping for.

Setting ourselves up for success begins with researching what expectations of us will be required and deciding if that is what we want to do. Once we have this understanding and meet these expectations, success will follow.

Individually, we can stand apart, like the repair man with the elevator. Becoming educated to do what no one else can means businesses depend on us for success. It is important to know that when you have the tools, you must also work well with everyone and be a team player. When we lift up other employees and empower them to succeed, then the company will continue to succeed. Doing what is expected of us efficiently and with a humble attitude creates an environment for growth, and when we stand out by helping the company grow, everybody becomes successful. There is always room at the top for everyone, always leaving one task that only we can do, and not giving away all our secrets is wise. Still using them to help others is the right attitude, and it will be noticed.

My communication skills and ability to connect with customers and the details of their accounts meant I was promoted to run my own division in a medical gas department, and I was overseeing ten thousand accounts. This was a success for me at this stage in my career. I had never worked in medical gas before, and I learned a lot about its purpose and the company I worked for. It brought my ambitions to be successful to fruition and put them to work.

I even researched how to bring in new customers and help my department grow and was very successful in doing so. I had come to understand the goals and created a way to make them happen, and it did.

I knew how to handle upset "hot" customers, and often, they were transferred to me to help settle their disputes. I knew the process and quickly grabbed details, making me the right person for that situation.

Success will come when we choose what success is for us and work to obtain it. It is okay to raise the bar of our own successes from time to time to continue to help us grow for a better future and opportunities. In fact, I highly recommend it.

Professionally

Way back in the beginning of time, working had different conditions and negotiations. We paid for labor daily with cash or some kind of bargaining. Some workers showed up in the morning to see if work was available. They would come to an agreement about how much they would get paid for the work required for a day's labor. For this story, let's say they received two pennies for a day's work.

One day, at seven in the morning, they are hired, and off they go into the fields. At about three in the afternoon, the foreman of the field sees that they are falling behind. Soon, a few new men came along to see if there was any work to be done. The foreman takes this opportunity to add workers. They negotiate a price, which is two pennies, for the few hours left in the day's work. Wait? The morning guys got two pennies for a full day's work; now, these guys get the same for a half day of work.

The morning workers began to protest as they felt this was unfair. Are they right to feel cheated? Both parties made an agreement to work for the amounts negotiated. While it may not be equal, it is fair. The negotiation that each party accepted was contractual. The foreman's job was to complete the job. How that was accomplished was completely within his control. We all may not get paid the same, but that is ultimately on us.

The farmers would take their eggs to the market to sell and trade for goods that helped keep their farms going successfully. I wonder what a basket of eggs could get you. I love fresh eggs, and their value to me is great. Did the vendors at the markets have favorites for buying eggs?

My mind often wonders about how business transactions were done back in those days, and it is a small hobby of mine. I read and research as much as I am able, and while this seems different to many, the connections between today's transactions and the ones from hundreds of years ago are not so different.

The owners of the business were mostly honest and treated staff with respect and value. Their reputation at the gates of the community was important, and they made extreme efforts to maintain their image.

Imagine being the owner of a vineyard; I have always been interested in the idea of miles of grape vineyard. I am sure that this has everything to do with my love of plants and my desire to create and invent. These were also the individuals that made up the community and regulated how it was operated.

Getting any business to see our value will direct us to places where our abilities can be put to the good of others, and the business is challenging. The people who complained about their value in our scenario have left a path of contention, and the foreman may not be willing to repeat employment with them. Had their responses been more accepting of the situation, the foreman would have taken notice and could have perhaps paid them more the next day, making up for any lost pay they may have missed out on.

Instead, they left an impression that may cause the foreman to be concerned about future employment. We must know how to take the blows and keep our best foot forward until there is a safe time and place for us to process what we deem to be unfair situations.

In today's environment, nepotism is alive and well. I have personally watched nepotism destroy people, businesses, and reputations in companies, communities, and churches. I get it; it is easier to interrupt family or favorites. I am way more comfortable inconveniencing my family with certain items than I would lay on a friend or co-worker. In business, when in the power of hiring someone, it often is family or friends that are hired.[15] Companies have gone to great lengths to make sure that families don't work in the same departments, and when done right, we can help our families. My personal experience caused the office in which I worked to become hostile to the person hired, not due to qualifications but due to favoritism.

If the situation is truly unfair and unwarranted, then finding the best solution to resolve it with respect and grace for the best result. If we are not able to change direction, there is always the next time for us to stand apart and make sure we value ourselves accordingly. Never settle for what others may say is your worth.

We often find that the person who is trying to solve the situation becomes the target. Accountability is a difficult action as it brings into light uncomfortable actions that need to be resolved. Like, who broke the coffee cup and glued it back together?

I love it when I catch my pups. I can tell which one chewed up the item as it is always the one hiding. Their sweet face of confession is working hard not to receive any consequence for the behavior. Fortunately for them, they never seem to get any. They get loved and understood. They are, in fact, dogs, and dogs do what dogs do. I should not have left out whatever tempted them to act like a dog.

Fighting both nepotism and accountability takes courage and tactics. Establishing a clear hiring practice and fostering a merit-based culture based on performance ensures diversity and monitoring the hiring process. For accountability, we want to set clear expectations, have open communication and active listening, and provide constructive feedback through honest conversations. When you give others the space to take accountability without consequences, they will. Actively working towards the solution while acknowledging the situation is a road less traveled but nonetheless a valuable one.

While I understand we need to work to survive for life, we also need to know our value and make sure that it is accurate. Yes, we may need to negotiate; however, having the information to back up our value is important so that we can show we have the knowledge to show our worth.

We live in a fast-paced world compared to only a few decades ago. People are, by and large, more brazen and willing to push the boundaries of business on both sides of the counter. Customers want to be treated better and want more in return for their money.

Businesses are trying to survive in an ever-changing technological world, trying to keep up with customer demands and loyalty. We know that only about one in ten customers will call to make a complaint.[16] With the internet at their fingertips, customers can bounce from business to business until they find one that meets their expectations.

Knowing what customers are looking for and meeting that expectation keeps us ahead of the rest; however, knowing that keeps us on our toes, always attempting to stay on the cutting edge of what is available.

Here, everything matters. First impressions, websites, appearances, and responses. Business must always remain on its toes, never failing to be ready to catch one. The odds are a little like fishing. We can fish all day, and all we catch is an attitude.

How can I be ready all day? The first thought is to trust in your product or service. If your product or service meets the standards to make other people's lives better, then it is not about selling the product. It will sell itself. They are buying the person representing the product. Is it a person or a computer? How easy is it for them to get to the end of the process?

I often find that in businesses, the process is the highest turning point that most customers experience. For me, professionally, I know these complaints exist, and when that customer comes to me, hot and upset, I am ready to bring their storm into my calm and to get to the resolution for them.

As we gather the details through their rant, we will be able to gather the information we need to at least start the process of concluding what went wrong. Always say "thank you" over "I'm sorry." It will go further than one may realize. Showing gratitude and not making excuses will communicate to the customer that they are valued and that you hear them, and it will bring them peace to know that you will make it right to the best of your ability. Balancing out with protecting the company is as challenging as it comes. Knowing both sides and finding a happy middle helps both sides to continue to do business and leaves us with the reputation of knowing how to care for others in business and for businesses.

A lady once told me that when she answered a hot customer, she would find a reason to call them back due to some emergency. By the time she called the customer back, they were more concerned for her and what she lied about than what their problem was. I disliked this tactic very much.

A tornado hunter must get in front of the storm to get information on how the storm works. Hot customers are much like this. All the information spilling out is now lost because they didn't want to deal with an upset person. Their integrity is now in question.

Our presence within our jobs, businesses, and positions gives us the platform to be the influential person who can change and support others' lives. It is how we approach each person, whether within the business or a customer choosing the business, that leaves an impression. How will that impression be received?

In one of my positions, the office I worked at was very rural. There were no quick convenience stores, and the company only allowed a thirty-minute lunch break. I requested management to create a "snack stand" in which employees could have a convenient way to grab something if needed.

Well, it was a huge success, making over five thousand dollars in the first year. It was well received by the staff and all the proceeds went back to the employees. I made sure of that. We would raffle off monthly incentives, and one year in particular, the business was struggling. The owner announced there would be no Christmas party. I again went to my management and explained that the snack stand had enough proceeds to put together some kind of Christmas celebration. And so, it did.

That little stand did more than provide quick snacks for employees in the office. It helped the drivers and the customers.

When they came into the office, they purchased snacks while they waited for service. It had become a staple, and with that, it boosted morale among everyone. Amazing what a little food could do.

Success in our surroundings comes from within the individuals with the courage to open the big red door of life and see what lies behind it. Let go of the uncertainties of believing we are not enough to make the change. When we share our ideas and ambitions, the direction in which we see success can impact others and lead them to success as well.

Spiritually

A warm furry blanket wrapped around me, cuddled up by the fire with a cup filled with joy. The peace and quiet of a crackling fire or light music with a peaceful feeling holding me tightly. The spiritual side of life is the self-care moments where and how we decompress.

We all have different preferences regarding how we find this peace and calm within our inner selves. It is like hitting the reset button from a day or days of work, life and the hectic overwhelm of survival. Having our nails done or hair fancied up and shopping for new clothes helps us to feel good about ourselves.

Resetting deeper inside us equals the balance of our personal seesaw of life. The weight of our spirit must balance that of life's hardships and troubles.

I always think of the plate of tasks that I carry to be more of a platter. Balancing out the "asks" and needs of family, friends, and career tends to be challenging. I am a people pleaser. No matter how much I want to please people or myself in the growth of reaching my goals and setting my bar for success I can only limit myself to that which I can obtain at a healthy level.

Becoming overwhelmed by tasks only leads to more stress and potential failure. As we described earlier, with the wheelbarrow analogy, I don't like using the word "no" for an answer when someone is asking for a favor or assistance. I find it to be discouraging and rejecting.

There are ways to communicate around no: deflecting to another solution that empowers the person to handle it themselves, suggesting services offered by other sources that specialize in their need, and even attempting to put it off until another time frame when my schedule will allow me to be the one that assists. I work hard not to have to come out and say no all the while.

There are many moments in life where individuals will ask for assistance when in fact, they are completely able to handle the situation themselves. It isn't that they can't do it; often, it is the act of doing it independently that is the struggle. My husband is one of this nature. He can do many things independently; however, he likes my company, so I comply with his request. He is my husband and my main customer; therefore, making sure he has my attention is important to me.

This is the part of spiritually that is also accountability. Standing on our own two feet to accomplish what we want is difficult, and we tend to want to pull someone in with us. Two are stronger than one, and the more we add, the more strength there is. The rope is layers of string. Breaking one string is easy; by putting ten entwined together, they are not so easily broken. This is how we find support on our spiritual side. We join with like-minded individuals, so we are more successful. Teams are extremely important in the success of certain areas of life. The baseball team having nine players on the field increases their chances of success. The more we have covered the field, the less likely the other team can score.

That space in the middle of us that often feels empty is meant to be filled with our spiritual side. No matter what we attempt to put in that void, it will never measure up until we find the spiritual solution that is meant to be there. It is like a puzzle piece. Only one piece fits; we can't force the wrong piece to go where it doesn't go.

Faith is what fits best into this space, faith in what you ask. You get to decide that. Let's use an example of faith. When I walk into a room and flip up that light switch, I have faith that the lights will come on. I am counting on it, and it doesn't let me down. Faith is complete trust or confidence in someone or something.

Faith is self-care already processed. If you have ever experienced the art of waxing, it is very interesting. When a statue or monument develops a crack, there is a wax that is placed in the crack so that it is not seen, and it holds the item together so that the weather or other outside elements cause no additional damage.

Well, that is faith. There is faith in the wax to hold it together. And it does what it is meant to do. There is a practice called Kintsugi. It originates from Japan, and when pottery is broken, they repair it with a gold powder mixed with a lacquer, and the piece is striking. The gold powder gives faith that the bowl will not leak. What is your gold? Is it striking when faith is displayed?

The delicate balance is what "spiritual" means to you. Our daughter enjoys listening to music and helps her decompress, and at night, she has a particular radio station she has on to help her sleep. She had faith that rest would come with the calming music.

Joy can be a part of it, but it is not the main source. The main source is what makes you feel whole. While joy comes from what makes us feel whole, joy in and of itself is not the main source of feeling complete.

My husband adds to my joy greatly. However, he is not my joy completely. Relationships, by and large, don't make up this void either. While relationships add so much to our worlds, for good and bad, we are not defined by them.

What is the anchor that holds you in place and keeps you grounded? As I'm sure you have seen by now, Bible verses are my anchor. They are the words or poems that settle my core and fill the void deep inside me. While I don't say that this is for everyone, as I am aware that everyone can have a different anchor, this is what brings me great fulfillment in life.

I rest on words and mindsets to maintain my focus and keep me centered when life is swirling around me. When individuals, customers, or employees come at me with discontent, I can separate my emotions using my center balance so that I can clearly address them.

No matter what you find in this center of spirituality, it is the biggest part of self-care that is required to maintain balance. Keeping our spirit settled keeps our emotions balanced and opens doors for success in our relationships, careers, and lives.

This is where we never lose our tempers or become short with anyone. This is where I work to show others the options of how to do as I do. In addition, I use the shelf of experiences with life and trauma to reach my success because I know how to respond to many situations at a moment's notice.

Whenever I pick up a book or watch a movie, I gain a great expectation of what it will add to my life and to my emotions and how they will support my spirit as I carry parts of them with me.

There are books and movies that I read and watch repeatedly. I want to absorb the mindsets and gain the vocabulary that will assist me in navigating through life and business. I want to understand how to love people and help them feel valued and loved.

These treasures that line the shelves of my bookcases have become my friends in quiet spaces as they encourage me and motivate me to never give up on myself or the ones around me.

Once we are behind the big red door, there will be moments when we will stand alone as we wait for others to see and have faith that we can lead them to a safe place in life where they, too, will find success.

It is not abnormal for others to fear something they do not know. They may criticize us out of that fear and keep their distance. Let them take the time they need and continue the steady path of what you believe and know is the solution.

Once they see that our experiences in life are the same as theirs, they begin to listen, and the seeds we plant in their hearts with the mindsets of success will begin to grow.

Success

*1) The Elders which are among you I exhort, who am also an elder,
and a witness of the sufferings of Christ,
and also a partaker of the glory that shall be revealed:*

*2) Feed the flock of God which is among you, taking the oversight
thereof, not by constraint, but willingly;
not for filthy lucre, but of a ready mind;*

*3) Neither as being lords over God's heritage,
but being ensamples to the flock.*

*4) And when the chief Shepherd shall appear,
ye shall receive a crown of glory that fadeth not away.*

*5) Likewise, ye younger, submit yourselves unto the elder.
Yea, all of you be subject one to another,
and be clothed with humility: for God resisteth the proud,
and giveth grace to the humble.*

*6) Humble yourselves therefore under the mighty hand of God,
that he may exalt you in due time:*

7) Casting all your care upon him; for he careth for you.

*8) Be sober, be vigilant; because your adversary the devil,
as a roaring lion, walketh about, seeking whom he may devour:*

*9) Whom resist steadfast in the faith, knowing that the same
afflictions are accomplished in your brethren that are in the world.*

*10) But the God of all grace, who hath called us unto his
eternal glory by Christ Jesus, after that ye have suffered a while,
make you perfect, stablish, strengthen, and settle you.*

11) To him be glory and dominion forever and ever. Amen.

1 Peter 5:1-11 (KJV)

Acknowledgments

Making sure I acknowledge everyone who helped me reach the goal is the challenge when saying thank you. The list of individuals that lifted me up through the decades to get me past the finish line is wide and deep. This effort to express my gratitude to all who have supported me and assisted me will certainly fall short, but know that I appreciate you all; from the beginning to the end, all of you have my heart, and I am truly grateful.

While suffering themselves, my parents secured the foundation for me so that I could be molded into the individual I am today. They inspired me with the lessons that I learned and gave me the understanding that guided me through some tough times of my own. However, I was prepared to meet those days, and for this, I am thankful that even through their struggles, they were amazing parents who loved me deeply and always cheered for my dreams to come true and to be successful.

Supportive, generous, kind, and loving would describe my best friend, my love Jeff. For decades, he has listened to my wild dreams and crazy adventures and always supported them. While they didn't all come to pass, he never faltered at being the ear, shoulder, and heart that I needed to maneuver through what life would become. My admiration for and dedication to Jeff will never cease and I will forever be by his side, my number one person in this world.

The lessons of motherhood from all three of my children are invaluable to my heart. I soaked up every moment of their lives, learning how to give them the space to become the individuals they are today. I loved watching them make choices and being the one who helped guide them through their years from toddlers to adults, along with sharing this amazing role with my best friend, who gave so much kindness and wisdom to their lives. I love that they are individuals, and one is not like the other. They have their own personalities and ambitions with loyalty and care for others.

My extended family of grandparents, aunts, uncles, and my two daughters-in-law brought so much peace to my heart to know that my sons would have the same teammate as I have in a spouse. My grandparents' lessons from the time of the depression were knowing how to live within your means and the special recipes from grandma's Italian cooking and my Nana weekends with fresh peaches from her own tree. I am always so thankful for their unique influence on my life and the experiences they gave me for a lifetime.

Some very special people like Nona Prather, with her encouragement and wisdom, guided me through areas I had not yet been exposed to. Indie Books International, with Henry Devries and his team, have walked me through the writing process so that I can have a published book that I can be proud of. To Steve Swavely, PhD for his thoughtful words in our foreword. As important are the social media team, the director of photography, the website team, and the branding assistant Lisa Apolinski, who came alongside and guided me up and beyond for a better understanding of the journey.

To my closest friends, pastors, and mentors, thank you for listening and giving input and perspective to help me see that which otherwise I may not have. To anyone that I may have left out, thank you. As I stated in my opening, you all have my heart, and I appreciate all of you deeply.

About The Author

Angela Webber, aka Ms. Angie, is a nationally recognized customer success savant. She works with corporations with customer-facing teams to help them level up customer interactions so that the team and customers create loyalty and a better experience for both. She guides audiences and clients to move from traumas to success.

Her experience is involved in more than customer interactions but in the entire process for businesses to thrive, from helping staff understand their part in the success of the business to understanding the entire process of all businesses.

In her keynotes "Success Starts With You" and her specially designed workshops, Ms. Angie inspires and challenges attendees to become advocates of even the "hottest" customers. She teaches customer-facing workers how to not let their own past trauma drip like a sponge onto the customer and keep calm under pressure. This is Ms. Angie's first book of many.

Angie has been married to the love of her life, Jeff, since early 1987. Becoming a wife and mother all at the same time was a special gift that she didn't take lightly. Angie's faith is a key factor in her success. Having the balance of all three, personally, professionally, and spiritually, has given her an insight into people, businesses, and, most of all, traumas that need to be processed to help maneuver through life.

There is no Jeff without Angie and no Angie without Jeff. We are truly one in this life as we merged our dreams and personalities throughout our relationship. Jeff is a simple guy with a simple outlook and helps me to keep my feet on the ground. Our children are our greatest accomplishment, and, in a word, to describe us is "fun." We are very intentional about having fun.

Angie's passion is to help those in her audience who have not yet found the vocabulary to find their love, joy, and peace in life, business, and spiritually. Her goal is to help them escape hiding and find their happily ever after in all areas of life.

Learn more about Ms. Angie and connect with her by visiting msangie.org.

Jeff and Angie

Author's Notes

While I have had a hard life from the time I was born, I do not let it define me. It will take forever to continue working through and balancing my emotions. It has given me the ability to share, teach, and encourage others how to know and keep their balance of emotions that rule over them. There is very little I would change. I like me, and I love the me God saw me to become. Yeah, I am still growing and learning. Still, I like this road, I love the transportation, and I am so excited about where I am going.

Community plays a huge role in finding success—finding the group of people that support us and assist in finding those dreams and goals that become a staple in our lives. We find confidence and a wide array of other attributes that are helpful as we push beyond our struggles and jump over our hurdles.

If it were not for the Christian community that was put in place along my journey, I have no confidence that I would have reached the goals and success that I have reached today. The group of believers who believed in me was instrumental in my successes, no matter how big or how small. To all of them, I give a huge amount of credit and thanks along the way.

My best advice for every person seeking support and help is to find the communities that you need. There can be more than one; the key is that they believe in what you do and that you remain teachable and grow with the tools that have been afforded you. While they support you, they may not always believe in what you are doing. Ponder those challenges but never quit. Set a course correction if needed, but always continue on the journey.

If you take away anything from *Behind The Big Red Door*, I hope that you will take away all the possibilities that you have in front of you. There is always success and hope on the other side of the door.

Angie and her family on a summer retreat 2024

Praise From A Friend

"We could not help but be powerfully drawn to Angie's natural enthusiasm and eagerness to learn as much as she could in order to improve life for herself and her loved ones.

She began volunteering around our church and, before long, she was investing dozens of hours each week in our church office and elsewhere, eventually making a real and obvious impact in our faith community.

It is only natural that Angie should want to share her life story with others, both in celebration for a truly meaningful life that almost never came into existence, and also in the hope that her story might inspire her readers as well. In this endeavor, as always, I'm loudly cheering for her from the sidelines."

—DR. DAVID RIEKE DMIN,
ANGIE'S PASTOR AND FRIEND

Works Cited

All biblical references are from the King James Version of the Bible.

1   Mark S. Kiselica and Mandy Morrill-Richards, "Sibling Maltreatment: The Forgotten Abuse," *Journal of Counseling & Development* 85, no. 2 (2011),148–60, https://doi.org/10.1002/j.1556-6678.2007.tb00457.x.

2   Laura Langford, "Six Basic Emotions by Paul Ekman: List & Facial Expressions—Lesson," Study.com, updated December 21, 2023, https://study.com/academy/lesson/ekmans-six-basic-emotions-list-definitions-quiz.html.

3   Mayo Clinic Staff, "Chronic Stress Puts Your Health at Risk," Mayo Clinic, August 1, 2023, https://www.mayoclinic.org/healthy-lifestyle/stress-management/in-depth/stress/art-20046037.

4   Kenneth D. Kochanek, M.A., Sherry L. Murphy, B.S., Jiaquan Xu, M.D., and Elizabeth Arias, Ph.D., "Mortality in the United States, 2022," NCHS Data Brief, No. 492, March 2024, https://www.cdc.gov/nchs/data/databriefs/db492.pdf.

5   Sandra Meier, Manual Mattheisen, Ole Mors, Preben Mortensen, et al., "Increased mortality among people with anxiety disorders: total population study," *The British Journal of Psychiatry*, July 7, 2016, https://pubmed.ncbi.nlm.nih.gov//27388572/.

6 "An Average Person's Anxiety is Focused On…," Bible.org, Accessed December 19, 2024, https://bible.org/illustration/average-person%E2%80%99s-anxiety-focused-on.

7 Lucas Graham, "People Who Avoid Accountability and Seek to Blame Others Usually Display These Behaviors," The Vessel, February 24, 2024, https://thevessel.io/people-who-avoid-accountability-and-seek-to-blame-others-usually-display-these-behaviors/.

8 "Chapter 11: Personality (lecture notes), https://quizlet.com/901067260/chapter-11-personality-lecture-notes-flash-cards/.

9 UWA, "The Science of Emotion: Exploring the Basics of Psychological Emotion, " UWAonline.com, June 27, 2019, https://online.uwa.edu/news/emotional-psychology/#:~:text.

10 "86 Percent of Consumers Will Leave a Brand They Trusted After Only Two Poor Customer Experiences," Businesswire.com, February 2, 2022, https://www.businesswire.com/news/home/20220202005525/en/86-Percent-of-Consumers-Will-Leave-a-Brand-They-Trusted-After-Only-Two-Poor-Customer-Experiences#:~:text=.

11 Shep Hyken, "58% Of Customers Will Pay More For Better Customer Service," Forbes.com, April 27, 2022, https://www.forbes.com/sites/shephyken/2022/04/24/fifty-eight-percent-of-customers-will-pay-more-for-better-customer-service.

12 "86 Percent of Consumers Will Leave a Brand They Trusted After Only Two Poor Customer Experiences," Businesswire.com, 2022.

13 "86 Percent of Consumers Will Leave a Brand They Trusted After Only Two Poor Customer Experiences," Businesswire.com, 2022.

14 Biron Clark, "How Often do People Change Jobs? (And Why?)," Careersidekick.com, November 9, 2023, https://careersidekick.com/job-change-data/.

15 Patrick Proctor, "How to Prevent Nepotism in the Workplace," Business.com, November 26, 2024, https://www.business.com/articles/prevent-workplace-nepotism.

16 Laurie Morrow, "What's More Dangerous Than A Dissatisfied
    Customer? A Silent One," Marketconnections.com, Accessed December
    20, 2024, https://www.marketconnectionsinc.com/dangerous-silent-
    cusomer/.

www.ingramcontent.com/pod-product-compliance
Lightning Source LLC
Chambersburg PA
CBHW022044210326
41458CB00071B/128